Reproduction

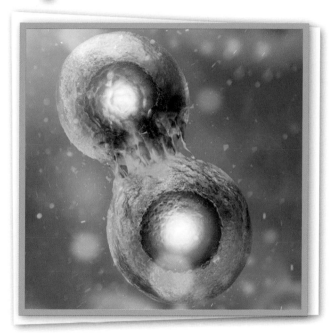

by Ruth Owen

Consultant: Jordan Stoleru
Science Educator

BEARPORT
PUBLISHING

Minneapolis, Minnesota

Credits

Cover and title page, © solvod/Adobe Stock; 4–5, © LeManna/Shutterstock; 5, © Arastoo Ahmadi/Shutterstock; 6, © Fotos593/Shutterstock; 7, © Japan's Fireworks/Shutterstock; 9, © ecliptic blue/Shutterstock; 11, © Bonnie Taylor Barry/Shutterstock; 13, © Designua/Shutterstock; 15, © Giovanni Cancemi/Shutterstock; 17T, © Niguella/Shutterstock; 17B, © Christopher Mansfield/Shutterstock; 19, © Designua/Shutterstock; 21, © lkordela/Shutterstock; 23, © Damsea/Shutterstock; 25, © Firn/Shutterstock; 27, © Claudia Paulussen/Shutterstock; 28TL, © Wasuta23/Shutterstock; 28TR, © Olga Vasilyeva/Shutterstock; 28ML, © Sashkin/Shutterstock; 28MR, © Daniel Prudek/Shutterstock; 28BL, © Dermot68/Shutterstock; and 28BR, © Flower_Garden/Shutterstock.

Bearport Publishing Company Product Development Team

President: Jen Jenson; Director of Product Development: Spencer Brinker; Managing Editor: Allison Juda; Associate Editor: Naomi Reich; Associate Editor: Tiana Tran; Senior Designer: Colin O'Dea; Associate Designer: Elena Klinkner; Associate Designer: Kayla Eggert; Product Development Specialist: Anita Stasson

Library of Congress Cataloging-in-Publication Data is available at www.loc.gov or upon request from the publisher.

ISBN: 979-8-88822-035-1 (hardcover)
ISBN: 979-8-88822-227-0 (paperback)
ISBN: 979-8-88822-350-5 (ebook)

For more information, write to Bearport Publishing, 5357 Penn Avenue South, Minneapolis, MN 55419.

Contents

A New Season

In spring, fresh buds pop open from bushes and trees. Flowers poke their way through newly green grass. Young chicks chirp in their nests, and little calves tramp through fields. The world is full of new life as the season changes.

Some animals build special homes for their babies. This keeps the young animals safe from harm. Birds make nests. In these small, tucked-away beds, birds care for eggs and chicks.

All living things **reproduce**. Animals, plants, and other living things make copies of themselves.

Animals have young and plants make new plants. As they die, the younger life grows. Soon, this life makes even more life and then dies, too. The cycle continues, keeping life on Earth going.

When animals stop reproducing, they die out. There were once many Pinta Island tortoises. Eventually, only one was left. His name was Lonesome George. When George died in 2012, there were no more Pinta Island tortoises.

Reproduction Two Ways

There are two ways that living things can reproduce. These are **sexual** reproduction and **asexual** reproduction. During sexual reproduction, two parents come together to make new life. For asexual reproduction, a single living thing can make a copy of itself without another parent.

We call a human mom or dad a parent. But the word can be used for any living thing that reproduces. There are all kinds of plant and animal parents.

A New Life Begins

Most types of animals and plants go through sexual reproduction. Sexual reproduction needs to have one male parent and one female parent. Why? Because males and females have different special **cells**, or tiny living parts of themselves.

Living things can reproduce only with their own kind. An oak tree can make new life with another oak. It can't reproduce with a pine tree. Likewise, an elephant and rhino can't have a baby.

Sometimes, male and female parents look different.

Making a Living

The parent cells used in sexual reproduction are made during **meiosis** (mye-OH-sis). Meiosis starts off with a special type of female or male cell. The cell divides into two, then divides again. In the end, there are four cells, called **gametes** (GA-meetz). Each gamete has **genes**, or special instructions to make new life.

Before a cell splits during meiosis, it makes a copy of things inside itself. When it becomes two, each new cell gets the same set of parts that were in the first cell.

Meiosis

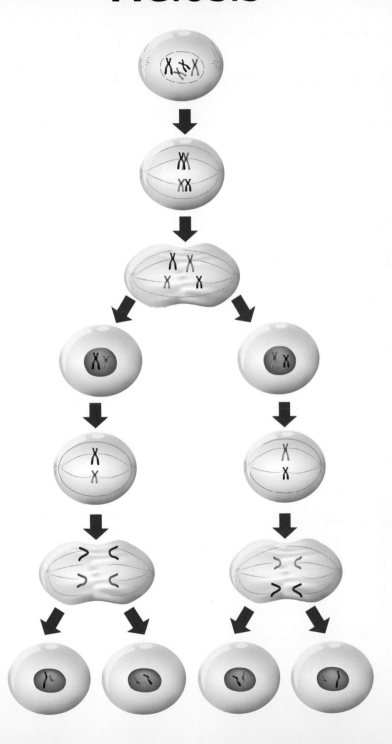

Any new life that comes out of sexual reproduction gets half of its genes from a male gamete. The other half comes from a female gamete.

In animals, female gamete cells are eggs. The male cells are sperm. Plants have egg cells, too. The male gametes in plants are called pollen.

A person might have a face a lot like their mother's. They may be tall and have red hair like their father. That is because they got genes from both parents.

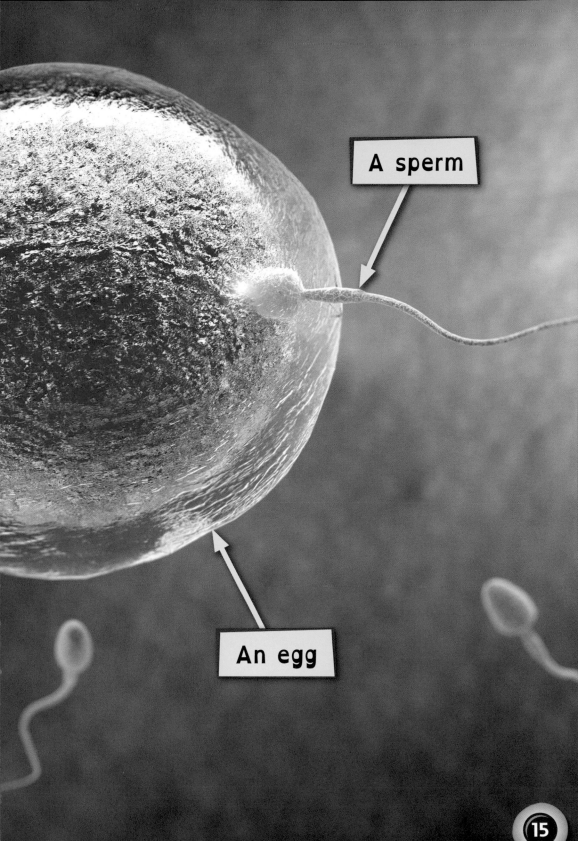

A sperm

An egg

Celling Life

When a female and a male gamete join together, the egg cell is **fertilized**. For many animals, sexual reproduction takes place inside the female's body. Sometimes, the eggs and sperm join up outside of the animals' bodies.

Human reproduction takes place in the female's body. Some frogs do things differently. They send their eggs and sperm into ponds and other bodies of water. The eggs are fertilized in the water.

Once an egg is fertilized, the cell starts to make more cells. It does this through **mitosis**. The cell makes copies of itself and then splits into two cells. Those cells divide again, and the following cells keep dividing. They become many cells. Together, all these cells will become a new plant or animal.

What makes meiosis and mitosis different? Mitosis can go on forever. It makes many copies of all different kinds of cells. Meiosis only happens with special cells. It stops once there are four gametes.

Mitosis

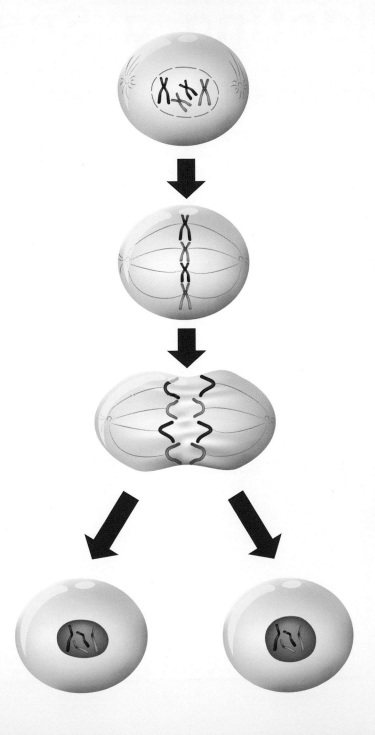

Planting a Seed

Some plants go through sexual reproduction, too. They may grow flowers with pollen and eggs. Pollen can join with eggs if the wind blows them around. Bees and other animals that eat from flowers may move pollen, too.

A fertilized plant egg becomes a seed. This seed can grow new life.

Some plants grow seeds in their fruit. An animal may eat the fruit and poop the seeds out later. The fruit may drop from a plant and roll away. This helps plants spread their seeds.

Pollen

One Becomes Two

Some living things go through asexual reproduction. A single parent copies itself. Sometimes, a parent can fertilize its own egg to make new life.

Things may go through mitosis to reproduce asexually. A single cell splits into two. These cells go separate ways as different living things.

Some sea stars can go through asexual reproduction. If a piece of the animal's body breaks off, the piece may keep on living. It grows more arms and becomes a new sea star!

Some plants and animals can make new life in multiple ways. Daffodil plants grow flowers with eggs and pollen. They mix and make seeds to reproduce sexually.

Under the ground, daffodils reproduce asexually. They can grow a tiny new bulb from a parent bulb. The little bulb becomes a new plant.

Honeybees, snakes, fish, and lizards usually go through sexual reproduction. However, some single animal parents have made babies alone. This can happen when it is hard for a female to find a male parent.

A new bulb

A parent bulb

Reproduction for the Future

Why reproduce one way or the other? Sexual reproduction mixes genes. This gives new life more chances to get what it needs to grow strong and healthy. Asexual reproduction can make life without things needing to come together. But whether with a single parent or two, reproduction is key for life on Earth.

A few living things can go through both kinds of reproduction. When there are fewer parents, they go through asexual reproduction. When there are many parent options, sexual reproduction may happen.

New Plants and Baby Animals

Most animals and many plants go through sexual reproduction. They get genes from both of their parents. Let's review how this works!

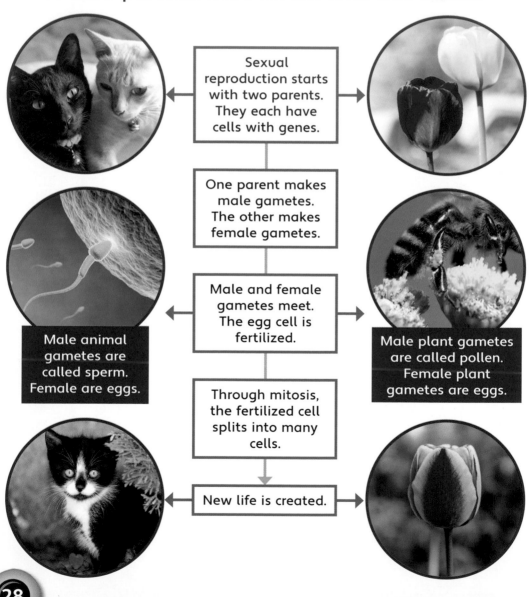

Sexual reproduction starts with two parents. They each have cells with genes.

One parent makes male gametes. The other makes female gametes.

Male and female gametes meet. The egg cell is fertilized.

Male animal gametes are called sperm. Female are eggs.

Male plant gametes are called pollen. Female plant gametes are eggs.

Through mitosis, the fertilized cell splits into many cells.

New life is created.

★ SilverTips for REVIEW

Review what you've learned. Use the text to help you.

Define key terms

asexual reproduction   mitosis

gamete   sexual reproduction

meiosis

Check for understanding

What is needed for sexual reproduction to take place?

Explain how meiosis and mitosis play a role in reproduction.

How is asexual reproduction different from sexual reproduction?

Think deeper

Do you think it would be good if every living thing could reproduce sexually? What about asexually? Why or why not?

★ SilverTips on TEST-TAKING

- **Make a study plan.** Ask your teacher what the test is going to cover. Then, set aside time to study a little bit every day.

- **Read all the questions carefully.** Be sure you know what is being asked.

- **Skip any questions** you don't know how to answer right away. Mark them and come back later if you have time.

Glossary

asexual a type of reproduction in which a living thing makes new life by itself

cells basic, very tiny parts of a living thing

fertilized made able to produce young

gametes special male or female cells that can join with other cells to make new life in sexual reproduction

genes instructions inside cells that determine how a new living thing will be

meiosis the process in which cells divide into four cells that can come together to make new life

mitosis the process of a single cell splitting into two identical cells

reproduce to make more of a living thing

sexual a type of reproduction in which living things join together to make new life

Read More

Gieseke, Tyler. *Plant and Animal Life Cycles (Earth Cycles).* Minneapolis: Pop! 2023.

London, Martha. *Cells (Discover Biology).* Minneapolis: Abdo Publishing, 2022.

Owen, Ruth. *Cells (Biology Basics: Need to Know).* Minneapolis: Bearport Publishing, 2024.

Learn More Online

1. Go to **www.factsurfer.com** or scan the QR code below.

2. Enter "**Reproduction**" into the search box.

3. Click on the cover of this book to see a list of websites.

Index

About the Author

Ruth Owen has been writing books for more than 12 years. She lives in Cornwall, England, just minutes from the ocean. Ruth loves to write books about animals and nature.